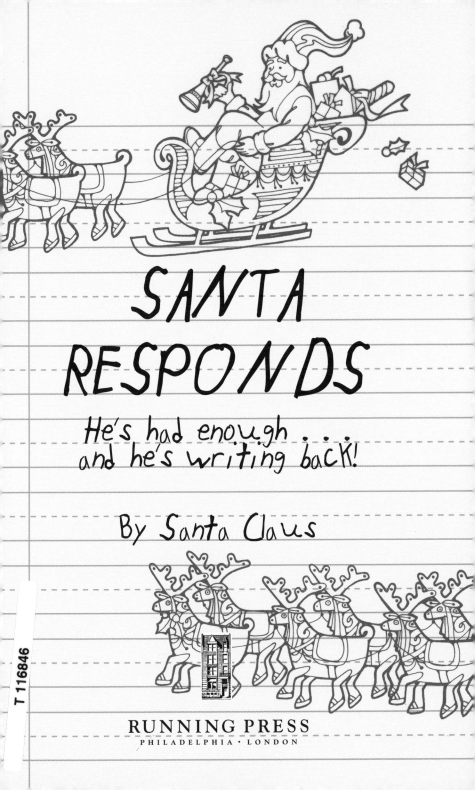

SANTA RESPONDS

He's had enough...
and he's writing back!

By Santa Claus

RUNNING PRESS
PHILADELPHIA · LONDON

© 2008 Santa Enterprises

All rights reserved under the Pan-American and International Copyright Conventions

Printed in Canada

9 8 7 6 5 4 3 2 1

Digit on the right indicates the number of this printing

Library of Congress Control Number: 2008927746

ISBN 978-0-7624-3089-5

Cover design by Matthew Goodman

Interior design by Matthew Goodman

Typography: times

Running Press Book Publishers

2300 Chestnut Street

Philadelphia, PA 19103-4371

Visit us on the web!

www.runningpress.com

Publisher's Note: Most of the letter-senders' names have been changed to protect the innocent . . . or preserve the illusion for at least another Christmas or two.

This is a parody. (As if the front cover wasn't a clue.) Brand names are still the registered trademarks of their respective companies. If you don't get this, you should probably not write to Santa other than to ask for a sense of humor.

Office of the Postmaster General,
North Pole Division:

NEWS

For release 10 a.m. Monday, December 25, 2008

For centuries children have written letters at Christmas-time.
Whether addressed to Santa Claus, Saint Nick, Kris Kringle, Father
Christmas, or any of a dozen other names, they were all meant for
one magical figure who lives at the North Pole. Within these letters
children poured out their hopes and dreams, their wishes and
wants, their questions and concerns. On Christmas morning they
would wake to find if these requests had been honored. And it was
the *only* way to know if their letters had actually been read.

Until now.

No one quite knows why it happened, or what may have made the
old man crack, but shortly after Christmas, letters began arriving
for these kids. First just one, and then a few scattered more, and
then a flood of them began appearing all across the world. For the
first time ever, Santa was writing back.

And clearly he had an awful lot to say....

Dear Santa,

I really want some pink ballet slippers so that I can dance really good in my ballet recital. Everyone else has new slippers and mine are all beat up, plus they're black because they are hand-me-downs from my sister. My mom thinks I don't need new ones, so I thought I'd ask you for them.
I always do my homework. Plus, my friend Amanda told me you didn't exist, but I didn't believe her, so I am really loyal. I would like those ballet slippers so I hope you think about all the good stuff I did this year. Say hi to Mrs. Clause for me.

From,
Lindsay

Dear Lindsay,

First of all, it's dance really *well*—not that you're likely to ever do so. To dance well requires talent, not new ballet shoes. Your mother has recognized your complete lack of ability and that's the real reason she hasn't gotten you new slippers. I would be remiss in superseding her authority in this regard.

I encourage you to continue to do your homework, particularly math, as you are destined to become a mid-level tax accountant, not a prima ballerina with the New York City Ballet. And your friend Amanda may know more than you think. Blind faith won't get you anything other than 4-5 years in a minimum security correctional facility for tax fraud when you're 43. It will come as a result of being "really loyal" to your boss when his accounting shell game is finally exposed.

Ho Ho Ho

Dear Santa,

This year, I have been a very good girl. I have done a
few bad things, but I help my mommy with the dishes all
the time. And I always say thank you, and so I deserve
lots of presents this year!
Please bring all of these things for me this Christmas
because I am planning on leaving you milk and cookies on
the table. I would like all of the Harry Potter sheets,
action figures and movies. Please don't forget to bring
a bicycle with pink ribbons and a basket too. If you can
only bring one thing, please bring a puppy—mom and
dad won't mind.

P.S. My little sister has not been very good this year
because she broke my headbands and pinched me, so if
you need extra room in your sleigh you can put my stuff
in instead of hers.

Thanks Santa!

Love,
Andra

Dear Andra,

A *few* bad things?! I think you seriously underestimate either your behavior or my intelligence. I'm used to kids trying to sell out their siblings, but rarely do they sink so low as to attribute to them the
misdeeds that they themselves are guilty of. We both know that *you*
in fact are the one who broke your sister's headbands and then
pinched her when she tried to tell your mother. This despicable tac-
tic may be useful for a politician, but you're not running for anything
here other than gift recipient.

   Which brings me to your wish list. I'm sick and tired of *Harry Potter*, and I don't just mean lugging the heavy things around. In case
you haven't noticed, it's the same damn story, book after book after
book. Who cares if the ancillary stuff is inventive when the plots
themselves suck?! The bookstores are filled with thousands of other
books, almost all of which are better written than any Harry Potter
title. Personally, I would recommend a series entitled *The Extraor-
dinary Adventures of Ordinary Boy*. They're just as much fun, and
will also show you how not to be such a sucker. Try reading some of
them. Oh, wait. That's right, they don't come with matching sheets!!

Grow up,

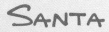

Dear Santa,

My big sister told me that you can see everything that goes on from the North Pole. That means that you can tell whether all the boys and girls in the whole world have been good or bad. I am writing you this letter to remind you that I have been very good this year. I just wanted to let you know in case you missed me because I am so small. I would really like to see your reindeer and give them some carrots, but I know you visit when I am asleep. So I wanted to help you out this year and tell you what I might like. I would really like some dolls and a new tea cup set. I also like stuffed animals, cats are my favorite. Merry Christmas Santa, see you soon.

Love,
Marisol, age 6

P.S.. keep an eye on my sister, she steals cookies!!

Dear Marisol,

You had me all the way through your letter, but then you went and blew it at the very end by ratting out your sister. What kind of a traitor are you? I know full well what your sister is capable of, but up until now, I never suspected how small and petty you could be. It saddens me that the lovely Wedgwood Tiny Tea Service I had set aside for you, and the giant-size stuffed Simba we've been working to complete for months will now be going to someone far more deserving.

Perhaps your sister.

Cheers!

Dear Santa,

Remember when I asked you for a microscope—as I recall I was pretty specific about the model and you sent me what amounted to a glorified magnifying glass, thus rendering the cool slides my sister bought me useless? No? Well, I DO. Somehow, even though I suspected that you didn't exist, I clung to the belief that you would come through for me, just once. I spent the better part of that year being quite "nice." When Kim Kempke called me names on the playground and threw dirt at me at recess, I just said, "Sticks and stones may break my bones but names will never hurt me." You and I both know what a brat that kid was, but I took it because I knew that you were watching.

When I got in trouble for taking the last Creamsicle, even though my SISTER had eaten it, I didn't rat her out because there is a pretty fine line when it comes to sticking up for yourself or being a snitch and yet there I was on Christmas morning trying to be gracious when I opened that sorry excuse for a microscope.

My sister and brother both gave me the same look they reserve for our cousin. You know, the one my Dad calls "simple."

I was heartbroken. What in heaven's name were you thinking? Was it a last minute gesture? I realize my last name is at the end of the alphabet, but I thought a kid would get some credit for taking it on the chin a couple of times during the year without complaint.

There were many times I wanted to be naughty, but the thought of losing out because I gave Danny Arico a charley horse was more than I could bear.

I weighed my options and realized that nothing would get in my way when it came to that microscope. Except Santa Claus himself, apparently.

Well, let me be the first to say that while you may have come through in years past, I am no longer your biggest supporter.

The word is out. People know that you are a fair weather friend and you have been marked lousy. Once that happens there is no way you can get back on my good side.

Not even if you brought me, say...a brand
new bike. It's too late, Santa.
It's not that I don't believe in you, it's that I
don't have much faith in your "powers."
So from now on, the gloves are off. Naughty?
You got it, buddy.
Let's see what you do with that.

Your friend,
Paige Warwick
a dissatisfied customer

P.S. And Kim Kempke? SHE got the Barbie
Dream House AND the Corvette. Justice? I
think not.

SANTA ENTERPRISES
NORTH POLE

Dear Paige,

When did you turn into such a little bitch?

Your friend,

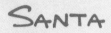

Dear Santa Clause,

I think that I have been very bad this year. Do you want to know some things I did? O.K. I'll tell you anyway. First of all, I have been planning to dominate the world. I've done other bad things also. That is the worst. Now, I will name some things that you will get me (or else). I want a giant machine gun to blow up the world with. I want a big evil Barbie doll. I want my own elf. If I don't get these then I will be extremely mad. So mad that I will blow up the world anyway. So Santa Clause, the world is doomed no matter what.

Hugs and Kisses,
Rianna

Dear Rianna,

I think it's time to see your doctor about taking you off of the Ritalin.

Calmly yours,

Dear Father Christmas,

Do you know some kid who might possibly fancy a little sister? My sister is always getting into my stuff and following me around. She always tosses her peas at me at dinner, and I worry she might throw her fork.
She draws in the books you gave me and got my fish water dirty TWICE!
I know I'm supposed to write you a list—you told me this at Harrod's, remember? So all that's on my list is:
#1—GIVE away my sister!!!!!!!!!!!!

Sincerely,
Giles

P.S.—I know my parents will be upset but I'll give them my fish to watch.

Dear Giles,

This is a common request of little boys. What you don't yet understand is that boys are given sisters for a very important biological reason, and that is to prepare them for the future torture of having wives. Women are maddening creatures and the only way that nature can make us ready for such a trial is to train us from childhood to cope with their aggravating behavior. Girls are saddled with brothers for a similar reason. Just be grateful you're not an only child. Marriage is often such a shock to them that they seldom survive it.

Your fellow bloke,

FATHER CHRISTMAS

(P.S. Whatever you do, DON'T let this letter fall into the hands of Mrs. Claus.)

Dear Santa

Santa why you din't get me

my little laptop. That is so kind

of sinning.

Mikey

SANTA ENTERPRISES
NORTH POLE

Dear Mikey,

Why you ain't writing in a language I can understand? Master English and you'll not only get a laptop, but you'll also avoid a lifetime association with the penal system.

Your homey,

Dear Santa,

For Christmas you gave me everything I wanted. I'm not sure if you gave my cat enough, but I think he can manage. I wanted to thank you for eleven whole years of fabulous gifts, and making a lot of children happy. I wish you would have eaten the cookies my mom set out for you. Your reindeer had no problems leaving my family a pleasant little present. Could you get down the chimney easily, we left a fire burning. There isn't much room left so I should get started with my gift demands. Next year I want A NEW CELL PHONE! A GIFT CERTIFICATE TO TIFFANY'S! EVERY NEW BARBIE ITEM PRODUCED DURING THE PAST TWO YEARS! A PLAYSTATION, AN X-BOX AND A Wii! A NEW OUTFIT FOR EVERY WEEK OF THE YEAR! AND A PUREBRED CORGI NAMED GISELLE! (if that's not to much trouble!!) By the way, next year, please bring my parents more things.

Thank you Santa!
Tara

SANTA ENTERPRISES
NORTH POLE

Dear Tara,

The signs were all there, but clearly you've missed them. The cookies weren't eaten, and the burning fire wasn't a problem for the simple reason that I've never stopped at your house—not even once. I don't even want to think where the "present" in your yard that you attribute to my reindeer came from.

I've never visited your house because your parents buy you everything you've ever even glanced at, all in a pathetic attempt to purchase your affections—little good that it's done them as I've watched you grow into an increasingly nasty, greedy little brat. If you had even a hint of a conscience, you'd realize that your parents receive little at Christmas for the simple reason that they have no money left after spending it all on you (and your cat). Frankly, it serves them right.

But don't worry, they'll continue to lavish money and gifts on you for everything from prom, to your sweet sixteen party, to your $500,000 wedding that they'll mortgage their house for. When your father has a heart attack, he'll even understand that your nail appointment took precedence over visiting him in the hospital—even though you'll miss your last opportunity to see him alive. There will be nothing left for you to inherit, but that's okay because you'll be married to a sucker who will work his ass off in a fruitless attempt to try and satisfy you. Through it all you will continue to feel deprived. By then you'll have even stopped noticing that I've never paid you a visit.

Coal is too good for you,

Dear Santa,

I hope you remember me from when I came to sit on your lap at the mall, but it's me Sarah!!!
I've been soooooooooo good this year you wouldn't believe it. I brush my teeth everyday and I listen to my mom and dad all of the time. I really hope you noticed. Say hi to Rudolph for me, I like him the best. Anyway, this year for Christmas, I really really really want a new Barbie doll and a make-up kit so I can play dress up with all my friends. I really hope you get this letter, Santa because I sure could use all of these things. Thanks again.

Love,
Sarah (with an H)

ps. I wont forget to leave your favorite chocolate chip cookies and a tall glass of milk, plus I got carrots for all the reindeer.

Dear Sarah with an H,

I'm afraid I can't say "hi" to Rudolph for you. Rudolph doesn't exist. He was an invention of the Montgomery Ward company back in 1939, and I've never seen a dime of the revenues generated by that red-nosed cash cow. Of course, that hasn't stopped every kid on the planet from writing me to ask about him.

As for your request for a Barbie doll and make-up kit, I hate to break it to you, but neither you, nor 97% of your friends are ever going to develop a body similar to that of a Barbie doll. And trying to achieve that look with make-up will just leave you looking like a hooker. Instead, I'm going to bring you a Raggedy Ann doll which better represents your future body type. And don't be glum. Raggedy Ann at least ended up with a loving partner in Raggedy Andy. Barbie just ended up with that dickless fag Ken.

Thinking of you!

Dear Santa Clause,

How are you? How are all your reindeer? I'm doing great because I've been so good this year. I share all my toys with my little sister and I wash behind my ears. I've even started helping grandma bake cookies especially for you! Since I've been so good this year I thought you might like to have my Christmas list. For Christmas this year I would like:

1. a new Playstation
2. Monopoly
3. Spiderman
4. a trip to Disney World
5. rollerblades

That is all for this year, hope to see you soon.
Lane

Dear Lane,

Consider this as a bonus tip from me. When sending a letter asking for free stuff, it pays to spell my name right—unless you really were trying to contact Tim Allen. (Depending on the outcome of my trademark infringement case against him and the Walt Disney Company, you may not do so well going down that route.) But let me continue on to the heart of your letter.

You truly are delusional.

I know you honestly believe that the good deeds you rattled off represent your behavior for the entire past year, rather than the activities that occurred during the two hours leading up to the writing of this letter. Two hours of good behavior hardly justifies a new Playstation, let alone a trip to Disney World!! It does justify a copy of the Spider-man edition of Monopoly, though, which combines two of your requests into a single crappy gift. You've earned it!

Your pal,

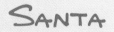

Dear Santa,

I'm sorry. I can explain.

-Your BIGGEST fan

Adele, third grade

Dear Adele,

Yes. I know you can. However, you might as well save your breath because I'm not buying it. And just so you know, it wasn't the fact that you stole the little baby Jesus figure from the nativity scene in front of your church and replaced it with a two-liter bottle of Sprite. I actually thought that was pretty funny. And it wasn't even the prank with your father's glue gun and your mother's diaphragm. What finished things off as far as you and I are concerned was the incident you caused when you told the little Pakistani girl in your class that when I come down the chimney of a house and find it occupied with non-Christians, I systematically execute everyone I find living there. Really now. What do you think it costs me in public relations dollars to neutralize that kind of slander? A lifetime of presents for my BIGGEST fan doesn't even come close to covering it…But it's a start.

Dare to Dream!

Dear Santa,

Can I have a new soccer jersey? All summer I liked to watch the soccer players in the World Cup and I think it would be really cool to have a jersey just like the pros. I like Arsenal and also PSG cuz the players can do awesome moves. I play soccer all the time, plus now I am on the A-team at my school and that means I'm pretty good. All the other guys on my team have jerseys from real teams and I want one to wear at practice. My coach likes it when we wear teams from England, where he is from. He calls soccer football but it's the same sport. Anyway, I bet lots of kids want jerseys, so I'll let you choose what team, as long as they're not bad.
Oh and my sister wants a tea set but she broke her arm so she can't write you a letter.

Thanks and Merry Christmas!
From,
Shamus, 9

Dear Shamus,

Maybe you should try a little honesty. Your sister didn't break her arm. YOU did when you attempted a mid-air karate kick against the Troll doll she was cradling in a bizarre attempt at nursing the thing. Her unintentionally hilarious action in no way justifies yours.

But I would expect nothing less from someone who is fascinated by soccer, or football, or whatever you want to call it. If there's been a more tedious and boring game invented, I don't know what it is. I travel everywhere (except to those nutcase Islamic countries) and it's quite clear to me that there's a direct correlation between the popularity of soccer and where that country falls on the sliding-shithole scale. It's no coincidence that the sport's popularity in your country has increased dramatically during the presidency of George W. Bush.

You can tell your sister she'll be receiving her tea set. You, however, will be getting nothing.

Merry Christmas!

Dear Santa (North Pole),

My big brother Tommy says your not real, but I don't beleeve him. I think your real. We have to prove him wrong, so this year I'm sending you my real Christmas list, and giving a different one for my parents to give to you. This is very important. Mine is the REAL list. This way I'll tell Tommy later and he will be wrong. Thank you, I been a good boy this year, heres what I want.

- Fun video game system & a game
- A new orange ball
- New blue clothes
- Baseball cards
- Computer games
- A electric instrument
- A pet named Spike
- Magazine prescripshun
- And suprise presents

Thank you,
Baxter

PS Remember, this is the RIGHT list. The list from Eddie and Laura Stevens is fake, so I can show Tommy your real.

Dear Baxter,

Well, you certainly are a devious little shit. It's too bad your "real" list wasn't as well thought out as your sneaky plan. I hope you enjoy the following gifts I'll be bringing you:

- an Atari 2600 System complete with Pong
- a pecan-crusted cheeseball from Hickory Farms
- a dozen blue girdles
- baseball cards for the starting line-up of the Scranton/Wilkes-Barre Yankees
- Quicken Tax Pro 2000
- an electric-powered-nose hair clipper
- a slug (name him Spike if you like)
- a one year "prescripshun" to the *National Review*
- and "suprise" presents consisting of everything you put on your fake list to your parents

Hope they don't suck!

Dear Santa (North Pol),

My momy says its taking me a reel long
time to think of my Chrismas list, but its
cuz I got a suprise that only you no about
Santa. My momy will male this letter to you
cuz I am at skool when the post offise iz
open (hint hint). I been very good this
yeer, so I think I shud get lots of
pressents. Heer iz what I want, I hope you
like momys cookees.
  -grean radeo control car
  -wii with games like basbal
  - a new grean sled
  -new gluvs
  -basbal cards
  -fishes and a see anenome
  -a mountan bike
  -futbal cards
  -sell phone
  -new books
  -legos and stuff

Your Friend,
Justin
PS Do you bemember me Santa? My name
iz Justin.

Dear Justin,

Of course I remember you. You've been writing to me for fifteen years now, and frankly, the acting like you're a small child gig is really beginning to border on the creepy. For the first few years, I just assumed you were an average, cute little kid just learning to write and spell. I got increasingly concerned as the years went by, however, and began to think you must have a slight mental handicap. That misconception was cleared up when I realized you were being home-schooled by your mother in your Little Rock trailer home. For the six or seven years that followed, I watched with curiosity to see when (or if) your mother would ever teach you to spell correctly. I was also fascinated to see just when she was finally going to stop bathing you. And here we are nearing your twentieth birthday and neither event has yet occurred. In that same way that even the most humiliating clips on You Tube eventually just become boring, I think I've finally seen enough. But I would like to thank you for this little peek at an average Arkansas family. I'm at last beginning to understand how the Clintons were able to initially get themselves elected.

Keep lurning,

SANTA

Dear Santa,

I have been a very good girl this year. I helped my little sister learn her ABCs and I helped Mommy set the dinner table every night! Mommy and Daddy say that you only visit good boys and girls so I have been trying very hard to be good. I think I have done a good job. I hope that I am on the nice list and not on the naughty list. If I am on the nice list, I would like a new doll with curly brown hair, just like me. If I am on the naughty list I will try to be more good I promise. If I am on the very good list, I would like a heart necklace like the one Daddy gave Mommy. If I am not on the very good list, I will try to be even more good I really promise.

Also, if I am on the very very good list, I would like a pair of ice skates too so Daddy and I can go skating on the pond. My little sister is too small for skating, so please don't give her skates too. Some things are just for big girls like me. If I am not on the very very good list I promise I will try to be good!

On Christmas Eve I will leave you my favorite oatmeal cookies that Mommy helps me make and milk that Daddy helps me pour. I hope you like it! Merry Christmas and stay warm Santa!

Love,

Beth 6

SANTA ENTERPRISES
NORTH POLE

Dear Beth,

I understand the desperation evident in your letter. However, your attempts to be very, very good, or "even more good" will do little to save your parents' marriage—just as your father's purchase of that diamond-studded heart-shaped necklace did nothing to gain your mother's forgiveness or assuage his own guilt.

I will of course bring you the set of skates you are hoping for. The solace they will provide during your weekend visitations with your father, though, will be minimal. It's hard to hear, but the truth is your parents will be better off apart. And you really must stop blaming your little sister for the failure of their relationship. You'll need her support in the years ahead.

With regret,

SANTA

P.S. I can't stand oatmeal cookies.

Dear Jolly Old Saint Nick,

I'm a 34 year-old father of two writing to you alongside my kids, Johnny (age 6) and Kirsten (age 9). We're all making our Christmas lists for you, and I want to show them that even adults get things from Santa if they ask. Kirsten is starting to wonder about you, whether or not you're real. I write to you every year, right?

For Christmas this year, here's what I'd like:
- Of course, world peace
- A good rate refinancing the mortgage
- the hybrid Ford Escape
- GPS navigation system
- Home Depot gift certificate
- a meat smoker
- Red Sox jersey
- new work boots

That should just about do it, Santa. Thanks for everything—I'll see you Christmas Eve after the kids go to bed, just like last year. I like those cookies, too!

Sincerely,
Trevor Innsbruck

SANTA ENTERPRISES
NORTH POLE

Dear Trevor,

You certainly do write to me every year, and every year you start off your list with the same old kiss-ass request for "world peace." But then you've always been the living embodiment of the phrase "talk is cheap." After all, why really do anything for the environment when you can get your self a "hybrid" and pretend you've done something without it inconveniencing you in the least. And go ahead and do all of your shopping at Home Depot, where you can't find any competent help to save your life. Meanwhile, the local hardware store down the street with the knowledgeable guy who would love to help you, will soon be out of business because his hammers cost a little bit more than Home Depot's. Local economies are being destroyed across your country because morons like you keep buying cheap shit at national chains that funnel your money out of your own communities, allowing them to wither and die. But of course that doesn't fit on a bumper sticker to plaster onto your hybrid.

Get bent,

Dear Santa Claus,

Hi, I am Colin Jacobsen. How are you? I am fine, just being really good like always.

Santa, what do you do when its not Christmas time? I know your really busy now, but what about in the summer? Do you go on vacation? Do you stay in the North Pole with Mrs. Claus? What about the elves? And what about the reindeer? Is Rudolph real? Do you have a pet polar bear? I want a pet polar bear, or a grizzly bear, or a lion. I like balloons. Do you like balloons? Can you make them into shapes, like bikes and giraffes? Why are there necks so long? Can you do magic? How do you read all the letters from all the kids and how do you eat so many cookies?

Do you really give coal to bad kids? I am a nice boy, I try not to be naughty at all. I like video games. I like kickball at recess. My mommy and daddy are nice. My sister Eva cries alot. I want squirt guns for Christmas. Mommy says no guns. I also like basketball. I need a new ball and a basket to shoot at when its warm outside. I want a snowboard too, but mommy says I'm not old enuff. Daddy says mommy worries too much. I want a pet turtle for Christmas too. I like the shell and daddy showed me his old ninja turtle action guys, and I like turtles. I think that's all Santa, I hope you can fly everywhere and eat lots of cookies.

Your friend,

Colin

Dear Colin,

Despite the stultifying repetitiveness of the questions I am asked, I do, in fact, like that kids ask them. Kids should ask lots of questions because it is, after all, the only way to get answers. If you ask questions your whole life, you'll continue to learn new things and become a wiser person. If you never ask questions you'll grow up to be a moron. (But don't worry. Your country's own recent history proves that that's no bar to becoming president.)

Of course, sometimes lots of questions are just the first sign of ADD.

Get help,

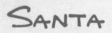

Hi Santa,

How is the North Pole? I live in Florida so I never see snow and it is always warm and hot. I hope that your reindeer can fly here without any snow. I will leave carrots for them to make them happy. I like carrots too but not more than I like candy. I don't think reindeers can eat candy.

For Christmas, I want a baseball so that I can learn to throw like my big brother. Maybe he will play catch with me on the beach like he does with his friends. I would like a baseball very much. It would be a good present.

My Daddy needs a new job because he lost his old one and my Mommy needs a new car because her old one is broken. Please see if your elves can help.

I will watch for you on Christmas Eve. My flashlight will be at the window so you can find my house. It is the yellow one with a white door just in case you don't see me.

Merry Christmas!

Ryan

SANTA ENTERPRISES
NORTH POLE

Dear Ryan,

You're a good kid. So it pains me to have to be the one to tell you that fate has dropped you into a cesspool—and I don't just mean Florida. The sad truth is that wonderful children are born all the time into families who don't deserve them, and with whom they don't deserve having gotten stuck. Soon enough you'll come to realize that your juvenile delinquent of an older brother is only your half brother. Steer clear of him. Meanwhile, the freeloader you both call your father (don't worry, he really isn't) will be moving on right after your mother loses her job because of having no way to get to work. Unfortunately, she'll soon begin a career that she can perform from home and additional half-siblings will be the result. Do not attach yourself to any of them. Make the most of the baseball I'll be bringing you this year. Your real father was the captain of the Duke University baseball team (enjoying a little Spring Break R&R) and you've inherited his brains and his talent ten times over. Pursue scholarships, and keep them a secret from your parasitic family. When you're accepted for a full ride at your father's alma mater, leave these soul-suckers behind and never look back.

I'm pulling for you,

Dear Santa Claus,

All I want for Christmas is a new bike. I hope the elves at the North Pole know how to make a bike for me. I want it to be blue. Blue is my favorite color. What is your favorite color? I think it is red because that is the color of your suit!

Shannon Riley Murphy says that you are just pretend, but she is always trying to trick me. I won't let it work this time. Please write back so that I can show her you are real. I believe in you Santa. If there is a bike under the tree on Christmas Day then you really must be real.

I don't need a helmet for the bike.

Your friend,

Masato

Dear Masato,

Don't you know that true devotion and belief don't require any physical proof to back them up? Of course that's exactly the kind of impossible-to-prove bullshit that leads people to blow themselves up for imaginary virgins and to believe that books written by sadistic desert nomads are the unchallengeable word of God.

In other words, good for you, Masato! If there's any advice I could give you it would be don't believe the claptrap that people like Shannon Riley Murphy will try to force-feed you throughout your life. Make 'em provide the proof. Of course, you could take that to an extreme. Such as a refusal to believe in the importance of, oh…say, safety helmets. But don't worry. Their importance will be made abundantly clear to you about seven weeks after you receive your beautiful new blue bike.

Enjoy it while you can!

Dear Santa,

I was very good this year and now it's payback time. Here is what you should bring me for Christmas:

- a new BMX bike (red or orange, with 4 inch alloy rims)
- money (at least $100, in small bills)
- snowboard (you know the one I want; it's the same one I asked for last year that you gave to Steve Alpher across the street by mistake)
- Puma glides (black and silver glow strips)
- an orange hoodie (not bright orange)
- remote control submarine
- a guitar (can you also arrange lessons?)
- anything else you can think of...

Thanks Santa. I know you'll deliver this year.

Tomas Murnz, 8

P.S. Don't forget: We don't have a chimney, so please use the front door!

SANTA ENTERPRISES
NORTH POLE

Dear Tomas,

You're a douche-bag.

Take it from me,

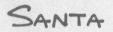

Hello Santa,

As I'm writing this I can't help thinking how dumb the world is. You completely disguised yourself. Living in the coldest place on earth using elves. Tell me, how much do you pay the mafia to keep you quiet? After all, an anagram for Santa is Satan. Hmm. How much would you pay me to be quiet? Just to show you I love you I'll take a European country, preferably Italy. I might as well rule the mafia too.

Sincerely,

(ME) Soon to be ruler of the earth (or at least Italy)

P.S. You know who I am.

P.P.S. And to all the stupid earth people, think about coal. How do you keep Hells firers running? Coal. So who would have coal? Satan. And who gives out FREE coal (no matter how expensive)? Santa. Think about it.

Obviously,

Faith, 5th Grade

P.P.P.S. Santa favors bad children since coal can be sold for money. While the good little kids sit around staring at the hot wheels cars the bad kids are buying million dollar estates. Hmmm. I wonder, Satan would favor bad kids. They end up lawyers.

SANTA ENTERPRISES
NORTH POLE

Dear Faith,

You're one of those smart people who just doesn't realize how stupid you actually are. You over-think every aspect of life to the point where you come to believe idiotic things like the Mafia killed Kennedy, aliens landed at Roswell, and the Iraq war wasn't about oil or petty revenge. You take moronic coincidences like my name being an anagram for Satan as concrete proof that it's true. The reason I leave coal for bad kids is that there's NOTHING a kid can do with just a single rock of it.

As less intelligent kids go on to be far more happy and successful than you, you'll become increasingly bitter and delusional, blaming everyone but yourself for the crappy place your life has taken you. So hold onto the lump of coal I'll be bringing you this year. If you're not successful at selling it to someone for a million dollars, let it serve as a reminder that the only person responsible for your life sucking is you.

You heard it here first,

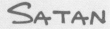

(oops…I mean Santa)

Dear Santa,
I need a new pair of pants because I ripped them and now I'm in my yellow polka dot bunny butterfly flower smiley face underwear.
From,
April

Dear April,

You only own one pair of pants? You have bigger problems than I can help solve.

Thanks for writing!

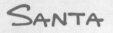

SANTA

Dec. 24, 2007

Dear Santa,

Hi I'm Kylie Barker! I was just wondering how do you get the presents? Do you order them? Do you make them? This year for Christmas I would like a Wii, Laptop, Webkinz, and clothes. Tell the elves, Mrs. Claus, and the reindeer I said hi! Have a nice BREAK!

Love Always,

Kylie

P.S. How do you get down the chimney?!

SANTA ENTERPRISES
NORTH POLE

Hi Kylie,

Honestly, don't you think you should have written to me a little earlier? A letter cobbled together on the afternoon of Christmas Eve is hardly going to get to me on time—especially given the incompetence of the US Postal Service. I once mailed a package in Manhattan that was addressed to my literary agent (look for my autobiography coming soon!) just thirty blocks away. It took TEN DAYS to get there!!

As for how I get the presents, I have them made in China just like everyone else. Their handwork is so tiny I'd almost swear they were using children to do it. And I'm not sure what they put in their paints, but the colors are so vibrant they almost make my head spin. Best of all, I don't have any of the labor union issues I used to have with the elves.

Take THAT, Toymaker's Local Seven!

Dear Santa,

Hey big guy, I've been waiting all year to write you this letter again. I hope you know that I've been a really good boy this whole entire year, well, except for the one time that I pushed Bryan down the stairs because he punched my best friend in the face. Bryan deserved it, so you can't punish me too bad, I know I was very wrong and I went to detention for three weeks because of it!!!

Anyway, this year for Christmas, I want only a few things. I don't want to be greedy because I know there's a lot of other kids out there that deserve more things than I do, you should give more to them than me because I got a lot of things last year anyway.

Starting with the biggest thing I want, it's this Tonka truck that I saw on this commercial once, it was big and yellow, and I could drive all my friends around in it; well, one at a time, but still. All the kids in the commercial looked very happy, and all year I was imagining one of those kids being me. The next thing I want is this really cool army hat I saw when I was shopping with my mom once. It's the coolest hat in the world, and I can't wait to get it!

The last thing I want for Christmas are these really cool power ranger weapons that are amazing. My friend Jory has them, and I play with them all the time, I think he gets mad. I want him to stop getting mad at me, so I really hope you can find them, or make them up at the North Pole...they are so cool. Once you see them, you'll know exactly what I mean!

Well Santa, I know my list is short, but that's all that I want this year. I hope you'll be able to bring me everything I asked for.

Thank you,

Mark

Dear Mark,

Don't you think you're a little old to still be writing to me? I mean, you're eighteen for Chrissake! And that wasn't a Tonka truck you saw in that commercial recently. It was a Humvee, and the happy guys you saw riding in it were doing an ad for the Army. That's where the cool hat comes in, too. And you'll be getting both of them even sooner than Christmas, minus the body armor of course. The National Guard program you joined to get out of sixth period study hall is rolling out to Iraq next month. Of course, you won't be armed with the Power Ranger weapons they promised you when you signed up. I actually have them up at the North Pole ready to go. Unfortunately, my bid to produce them for the Army was rejected, despite coming in lower than anyone else's. The winning bidder, Haliburton, should have them ready for you in about ten years—assuming you last that long.

Good luck!

DEAR SANTA,
I HOPE YOU LIKE MY COOKIES AND MILK CAN YOU NAME ALL
YOUR REINDEER TELL MRS. CLAUS HEY HOW ARE YOUR ELVES
DO YOU DECORATE OR DO YOU PUT UP TREE
BYE SANTA
MALI MCKEE
P.S. SAY WHATSUP TO YOUR REINDEER

SANTA ENTERPRISES
NORTH POLE

Dear Mali,

Punctuation is an amazing thing. Take the following sentence:

No presents will be coming this year for Mali McKee.

The insertion of just one single comma can turn this from being your worst Christmas ever to one of your best. What? You never paid any attention in school when they were teaching you about commas? Or spelling? Or basic punctuation? Well isn't that a shame?

Better luck next year!

SANTA

Dear Santa,
hello I am 9 and I would like 3 things
#1. A book set, #2.new arts and crafts, and #3
a couple webkinz.
How does your sled work? Did you know that
Christmas is my favorite holiday!
Love,
Liv 9

Dear Liv,

I'll be curious to hear if Christmas is still your favorite holiday after this year. As requested, I'll be bringing you the following:

#1 The Internal Revenue Service 1991 Tax Code (all eighteen volumes in the set!)

#2 The Junior Jackson Pollack Paint-By-Number Kit

#3 The carcasses of half a dozen insects I've carefully extracted from the spider web that hangs in the corner of my office

At age 9 you should know how to phrase your requests more precisely.

Ask and ye shall receive!

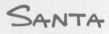

Dear Santa,

Hi! I want a puppy for Christmas. How do your elves make gifts? I hope I have been a good boy. I love my parents. Do you? Please come to my house. Do you like puppys? I hope I can see you!

You friend,

Henry Sellers

Dear Henry,

What an unusual question. Do I love my parents? To be honest, I really hadn't thought of them in years. Most people assume I'm an orphan thanks to the efforts of a publicity agency I hired back in the 1950's. They suggested going with the whole orphan thing as a way of mythologizing my past and creating an aura of mystery about my origins. The truth is that I did have parents. From an early age they trained me in the art of toy making. But did they ever let me play with the toys I created? No. They made me give them all away. Did it make me bitter? You bet. Did I take on the role of toymaker to the world in an attempt to win the favor of two nasty parents who ultimately would never be satisfied no matter how many toys I made and gave away?

   Now that I finally look at it that way, I see that what I've been doing is merely an attempt to gain the love of parents whose love was never attainable in the first place. There's no point in me making and delivering all of these toys. I see that now. Finally, I'm free of this onerous task. And I owe it all to you, Henry.

Free at last,

SANTA

PS: Whenever children ask me why I no longer bring them toys, I'll say it's all thanks to Henry Sellers of Evanston, Illinois.

Dear Santa,

I would like an iPod, MP3 player, 50 movies, and a Nintendo PS Lite. I also want a Game Cube. How do your reindeer fly?

Sincerely,

Adelina Forte

Dear Adelina,

My reindeer are able to fly because their muscles haven't atrophied from the inaction that comes from spending all of one's time on one's ass playing video games, listening to music and watching 50 movies. Maybe you should ask for some presents that require a little physical activity. It may do wonders in staving off the diabetes that will strike you at fourteen, and the heart attack that will bring you down at twenty. Laying off the donuts might help, too.

It's never too late,

COACH SANTA

Dear Santa,
I would like a Fender Electric Guitar
Laptop and Cellphone for Christmas. And
in school I would like good grades in
science + a little more freedom at home.
From,
Emily not Emma
P.S. Tell Roudolph I said "Hi"

Dear Emily not Emma,

As far as I know, Fender doesn't make an Electric Guitar Laptop, although it does sound like something I would like for myself if they do decide to produce one. Similarly, they also don't produce a cell phone, so I'm afraid you're shit-out-of-luck on those requests. If Rudolph existed, he might tell me that you meant to put a comma after the word Guitar, which would have given a whole new meaning to your wish list. But he doesn't exist. Sorry.

That brings us to your next request: good grades in science. Since science is increasingly irrelevant in your country, I'm not sure why you care. Your public schools have never exactly been on the cutting edge of science to begin with, and since they've eliminated everything from the curriculum that offends the various pinheads in your community, I think the only lessons left in your science books involve photosynthesis and gravity—although I suspect gravity will soon be dropped as well. Get it? Gravity…dropped! Oh, never mind.

As for your final wish for more freedom at home, good luck with that one. Your parents feel that keeping you a virtual prisoner will prevent you from becoming pregnant as a teenager. Of course, if they bothered to teach you any sex education, you'd be aware that the neighbor boy's attempt to give you a friendly "inoculation" against liberalism when you're fourteen will ultimately do nothing to actually save you from the welfare state.

Don't know much about biology,

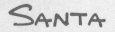

Dear Santa Claus,
In the song "I Saw Mommy Kissing Santa Claus" do you really kiss my mom? And thanks for everything last year. This year I really don't care about the presents I get. I care about the presents I give. By the way have a Merry Christmas, and a Happy New Year.
From,
Lucas, 8 and a QRTER

Dear Lucas,

I'm often asked this question, to which I usually reply: If I only had the time!

You'll get that in about ten years.

In the meantime, it's letters like yours that make me grateful that I can see within your heart. I often get letters from calculating little shits who feed me lines like "I only care about the presents I give" like so many beauty pageant contestants, and if I wasn't able to see the truth it would leave me in a difficult position. But I can see your sentiments are genuine, and it does warm my heart. I'll be bringing you a Game Cube and Wii this year, and I hope you have a ball with them.

And if I were to kiss anybody's mommy it would be yours.

Rrrawr!

Dear Santa,

How's the North Pole? Is Rudolph's nose still shining? I heard that Dancer had the flu and I hope the elves took good care of him so that he is all better by Christmas Eve.

I hope I am on your nice list this year. I know that I pulled my sister's hair a few times and ate candy when Mommy wasn't looking, but I think besides that I've been pretty good. Besides, Benjamin from my class is always pushing boys on the playground and every Christmas he gets lots of presents from you, so I think I should get some presents, right?

I really, really, really want a new puppy. I know that Mommy thinks I am not going to walk it enough but I swear I will. My neighbor, Josh, always plays with his dog in his front yard and I think it looks like fun. Plus I walked by the pet store yesterday and saw lots of puppies in the window, and then my teacher told us all about the dogs in the pound who need to be adopted. I would give the puppy a good home (I want a Golden Retriever, but a Beagle would be okay too.)

Thanks Santa. Look out for some gingerbread cookies at my house this year. They're my favorite so I'll save a few for you.

From,

Tristan

Dear Tristan,

It's really quite clever how you open your letter with some small talk, and then subtly slip in some minor transgressions as a distraction from the truly awful things you've done this year. Does "the pogo stick incident" ring a bell? Sadly, this tendency will serve you well when you make your entry into politics in your late twenties—much to the misfortune of the idiots who elect you. However, the attempt to further bolster your case by calling out the misdeeds of your class-mates is just piling it on too thick. Benjamin's aggression is merely a conduit for the latent homosexual tendencies that he has yet to even begin to understand. Not that it's any of your business.

After preparing your case in the most manipulative way possible, you finally reveal that what you want more than anything is a puppy. You claim you'd be happy with a dog from the pound. Well, I'll tell you right now, you're not going to be finding any Beagles or Golden Retrievers at your local shelter. What you'll find there are mutts. They're more loving, and definitely more intelligent than any pure-breds, but the truth is that doesn't really matter to you. In the super-ficial manner that will sadly serve you well throughout your life, the most important thing to you is appearance. The mutt that you are going to receive this Christmas will be loving and loyal right up to the moment three months later when your parents return it to the shel-ter because you've rejected it. A week later it will be put to sleep. I truly hope you rot in hell.

Jingle All the Way!

Dear Santa

How come you so
fat?

Love,

Ashton, aged 8

Dear Ashton,

How come you so rude? Seriously, haven't your parents taught you any manners? Or grammar?

If you really must know, I'm fat because I love bread, potatoes, pasta and booze. Those four things have been torture when it comes to maintaining a svelte figure. Now, some people may say I'm an incredible hypocrite the way I chastise others for letting themselves grow fat while doing nothing to maintain my own weight. It's a fair critique, but it's really a matter of apples and oranges (neither of which I like eating). You see, I'm immortal. I can eat all the unhealthy shit I want and it's not going to kill me. The same can't be said for any of the fat kids who write to me. So this really is a case of "do as I say, not as I do." I'm only thinking of them as I berate and ridicule them, all the while knocking back a bottle of Dewar's.

Life ain't fair,

Dear Santa,
Why does the Easter Bunny give us candy but we have to leave you cookies? That doesn't seem fair and mom says we have to be fair. Dad too.
Annabel, AGE 5

Dear Annabel,

If there's any lesson I can impart to you it would be that life isn't fair. While I applaud your parents' efforts to instill a sense of fairness in you, it really is a lost cause. As you get older, you'll find that the brown-nosers in your class get good grades with little effort while your perfect papers are only good enough for B's. In college, your whore-ish roommate will marry a millionaire while you date a pizza delivery boy. When you graduate, the incompetent ass-kisser who is hired the same day as you will ultimately become your boss. Through all of this, you'll whine that "it's not fair!"

It's not very well publicized, but the Easter Bunny is fully subsidized by the American Egg Producers Association. I make and deliver toys to millions of children every year, free of charge. If you don't think it's fair that I enjoy a few cookies for my efforts, then screw you.

I hope you're getting something good from the Easter Bunny this year, 'cause you're not getting jack from me.

Dear Santa,

I'd like to know some things. How do you fit in the chimney's? And if we don't have a chimney how do you get in.

And some of the things I wan't is wrestling figures or other things. Suprise me

PS: Hope you like the cookie's

From

Austin

Merry Christmas

Dear Austin,

It's never good to ask someone to surprise (as opposed to suprise) you unless you truly would be happy with anything you get, ranging from a West Hollywood Ken doll to a bucket of used hypodermic needles. Based on your one stated request for "wrestling figures," I'm guessing that you'd be disappointed in any kind of toy that requires intelligence or imagination to use. That eliminates a huge percentage of the toys on the market. I will try to do my best, though. My research has shown me that of the little boys who ask for "wrestling figures," 45% of them are future drug-using sociopaths, and another 45% are latent homosexuals. The remaining 10% are drug-using latent homosexual sociopaths.

I hope you enjoy your Ken doll AND your bucket of used hypodermic needles.

Your Best Buddy,

Hi Santa,

My sister is making me leave out oatmeal cookies for you even though they are gross. You probably like chocolate chip cookies better. I'll try to put some of them on the plate too. Please don't put me on the bad list, just my sister.

Looking out for you,

Kevyn

SANTA ENTERPRISES
NORTH POLE

Dear Kevyn,

You're absolutely correct. Oatmeal cookies are disgusting. The only thing worse are oatmeal cookies with raisins. At first glance, they look like oatmeal cookies with chocolate chips, and you think to yourself, *well, at least these oatmeal cookies have chocolate chips*. Then you pick one up and take a bite only to realize that they're really RAISINS! It's a joke of the cruelest kind. Hitler LOVED oatmeal cookies with raisins!

Rest assured that you will not be punished for this travesty. Your sister, however, shall pay.

Disgustedly yours,

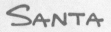

Dear Santa,

It's me again, Cate. Last year you bought me a lot of presents, and I just wanted to say thank you once again. This year, I want a lot of things, and when I say a lot, I mean A LOT. Mom says you won't be getting me everything I want, but I always tell her she doesn't know you like I do. For Christmas, I'll start out with some of the little things I need. I need a hair brush for Barbie and some new clothes for her too. She's getting very tired of the ones she's been wearing for the past three months. Also for Barbie, she needs the new dream house and the nice sports car I saw on the TV commercial, I think you know which one I'm talking about. Also for Barbie, she needs one last thing; these amazing new heels I saw last week in the store, they're blue and sparkly and they should fit her just right!!

As for me, I need a lot of things as well. I saw this really cute doll that I fell in love with. She had blue eyes just like me, and she also had long brown hair just like me too. Her name was Dress-Me-Up DeeDee and I saw her in the doll section of Toys R' Us. DeeDee is going to need some new clothes just like Barbie, except I hope they have some in a bigger size. DeeDee is going to need a new pink shirt, as well as some black shorts so she can match me when we decide to dress together. After DeeDee, I would like to get a friend for her to play with, so when she's home alone she doesn't get lonely. I found her friend in the same place as DeeDee, and her name is Julia. She looks just like DeeDee, except she has green eyes and blonde hair. I think Julia is going to want some new clothes too, so if you could bring her some, any kind you like, that would be cool.

Santa, I know this is a lot to ask for, but I believe that you can bring me all these things without thinking I'm greedy. I'm really not, even though my mom tells me I'm spoiled all the time. For the last of my presents, I would like my ears pierced. My mom always tells my I'm too young, but 9 isn't that young, all my friends have their ear's pierced and it's not fair! I think I should be allowed to especially since Natalie, my best friend at school, has two holes in each ear! Maybe you can take me without telling my mom, and then she'll have to let me keep them once they're in my ear! Natalie is just like me, we almost have the same exact things, except she has a little more than me, but its okay because we share most of our stuff anyway.

The very last thing I want for Christmas Santa, is a new bike to ride in the spring and summer. I want this yellow and green bike I saw also in Toys R' Us, dad knows what it looks like so he can tell you all about it. I can't wait to show it off to all my friends, I've never seen anything like it anywhere,

My friends will think I'm the coolest kid they've ever known.

Anyway Santa, I hope I get everything I ask for because in the past, I know you've always been faithful to me. If you can't get everything, then I understand, I know you have a billion and one kids to get things for anyway. I love you, Santa.

Love Always,

Cate F.

SANTA ENTERPRISES
NORTH POLE

Dear Cate,

You are greedy. You are spoiled. And your friend Natalie is a tramp.
Yet you're only a tenth of the torture you're going to be to others
when you get older.

I shudder to think,

Dear Mr. Santa,

I know there's lots of other girls named Krystal in the world so I think you got confused and gave me a Barbie when I asked for a Bratz doll. Can you switch them please?

Thanks,

Krystal

Dear Krystal,

That was no mistake. Despite what I think of Barbie and the message she sends to girls (and a few odd boys) it pales in comparison to what I think of the Bratz. These nasty, repugnant dolls are nothing less than the heralds of the end of civilization as we know it. You know what it says when a little girl says she wants a Barbie? She's saying she wants to be sweet, wholesome, and impossibly slim, and be loved by a pretty but androgynous boy. When a girl tells me she wants a Bratz doll, it tells me she wants to grow up to be an ignorant whore who will use sex to manipulate any man she comes in contact with.

 Mrs. Claus doesn't need any additional support.

Stick with Barbie,

Santa,
What's does ho mean? I heard it in a song and I
thought you'd know because you say it a lot.
Sincerely,
Franck, 9

Dear Franck,

I'm sorry. It's just too easy.

Dear Santa,
I'm going to leave you some cookies my dad
got at work and didn't want. The puppy you
got me peed on my bed again. Try to do better
next year.
Jessica Cehlar-Morrison

SANTA ENTERPRISES
NORTH POLE

Dear Jessica,

I know your parents always tell you to be honest, but, frankly, there is such a thing as being too truthful. People don't respond to comments like those you sent me by saying to themselves: "Oh, what an honest little girl she is!" No, what they say is: "Do you think Jessica is really that repulsive, or is she just too stupid to know better?" In fact that's exactly what I've asked myself, and sadly, the answer I settled on is that Jessica really is that repulsive. So this year, instead of toys or a puppy that doesn't pee, I'm going to be bringing you something far more precious. It's called tact. I hope you make the most of it.

Keep the cookies,

Dear Santa,
Please don't be mad but my Grandpa hit one of your reindeer with his car last night and even though he said it hurt his car more than his car hurt it I don't think it'll be good in time for Christmas Eve. My dad said you can borrow our dog Stinker if you need to because she's as big as a horse. I don't think Stinker can fly but she'll try her best.
Sorry.
Sam

SANTA ENTERPRISES
NORTH POLE

Dear Sam,

Don't worry. You're grandpa didn't hit one of my reindeer. Unfortunately, he did hit a jogger—despite his claim that it was a deer. I'm afraid the police will trace the incident to him by early Christmas morning. Just as you're all opening the gifts I've left for you, they'll arrive to arrest him for manslaughter.

Enjoy the presents!

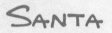

SANTA

Hey Santa,

This is my first time writing to you in the seven years that I've been alive. Dad says it's time to be a big girl and write my own letters instead of telling him what to write.

I want to start off by saying that this year, even though it was one of the hardest years for me, I was so good. It's so hard to be good, but in the end, I think it's all worth it. Me and my brother didn't fight that many times, but when we did, it was nothing too big. He fought with me once because I ate the last fruit roll-up. He hit me and then my mom grounded him. I tried to start a fight with him once, but then he told my mom and then I got grounded; that was really the only time I did anything wrong. Nothing else really happened that was big during this year. My oldest sister went off to college so she hasn't been around. I saw her a week ago for thanksgiving, but she wasn't around that much, she was too busy running around with her boyfriend. She comes home again in three weeks for a really long winter break, and to spend Christmas with us, so I'm really excited. She's my favorite sister in the whole world, and she always gives me anything I want. I don't think I could ask for a better sister.

Moving onto Christmas, I really hope you can bring me everything I ask for. I know it's a lot, so if

you can't deliver everything in one night, then I'll
understand a little bit. The first thing I want are
a lot of Barbies. I love Barbies. They're my favorite
doll to play with. When I get older, I want to look
and act just like her! At night, when I'm sleeping,
all I dream about is Barbie. Everything about her is
perfect, and I want to be just like her!
The other thing I would like to ask for are
a lot of Webkinz. You know, those animal internet-
talking pets? They're so cool. I think they're the
best thing that has ever happened to my computer.
I have the dog, the frog, the pig, and the moose,
so if you see any other ones that I don't have, I
would love them! I trust anything you chose for
me. I think I would like either 2 or 3 just so my
other Webkinz have other friends to play with!
The other thing I would like to ask for is the
Barbie dream car, and the Barbie dream house... I
told you, I'm in love with Barbie. The Barbie dream
car is so so so cool. It has automatic driving, so I
don't even have to do anything but be inside of
the car, and it's also very safe. My older sister
even thinks it's cool, so that says something. The
Barbie dream house is for Barbie. She needs to
move because she says her other house is getting
to small, so this house is the perfect size for her.
There's nothing else really that I want on
Christmas. I hope you can bring it to me. I will

leave some cookies and milk out for you like I always do, and if you don't eat them, it's okay because maybe your reindeer will get hungry. I'll leave an extra glass of milk out for them too. I hope you don't get too tired delivering all the presents to all the other girls and boys. Good Luck!

Love you,

-Emma-

Dear Emma,

You're one of those talkative kids, aren't you?

Try listening occasionally,

Dear Santa,

I already sent you my Christmas List, but I just thought about something really important and wanted to ask you a question. Can you please include the receipts with my presents? Last year, you made a couple of mistakes (I wanted an X-Box, and you gave me a Nintendo instead) and it would be really convenient if the receipts were included so I can exchange the presents I don't like.

Thank you, Santa,

Your friend,

Jason

SANTA ENTERPRISES
NORTH POLE

Dear Jason,

I'm afraid you've made the fundamental mistake of assuming my gifts are returnable and that I offer "receipts" for them. First of all, where do you propose to return these gifts? I doubt very much that Best Buy is going to honor a receipt from me even if I were to provide you with one. That would leave you in the position of having to haul your ass all the way to the North Pole to make the exchange. Practical? Not really. But if you want to give it a shot, I'll be happy to honor your request if you manage to survive the journey.

Dress Warmly!

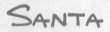

Dear Santa,

My mom and dad told me I'm spoiled and that I should think about the poor kids in Indiana because they don't have any toys and I should be thankful because I have toys and food and a nice house and they told me I should give all my presents to the poor children in Indiana but I don't think that's fair so maybe you could just bring me the toys from my list and give those kids all my old toys. Can you do that Santa?

Sin cely

Chris Eck

SANTA ENTERPRISES
NORTH POLE

Dear Chris,

While I agree that we should all feel sympathy for any child born in Indiana, I believe your mother actually said India—unless she didn't, in which case she's probably a moron. In any case, don't feel bad for the "poor" children of India. While their standard of living is still far below that of the "developed" world, they are catching up rapidly. By about the start of your second marriage (it will fail, too) India will have surpassed the United States in wealth and standard of living. You see, while all you Americans sit around complimenting yourselves about being number one, the people of India are actually educating themselves in real courses such as Microbiology and Quantum Physics—as opposed to made-up subjects like Creation Science and Hip Hop Culture. But don't worry, even as your standard of living slides inexorably toward the gutter, you'll still think you're number one—even if you don't know the difference between India and Indiana.

Thanks for caring!

Dear Santa,
Thank you for the presents that you gave me last year. How many elves do you think you have in your workshop? About 116,000? I don't know. Do you know what people are doing right now? Sorry for all the bad things I have done. What kinds of cookies does Mrs. Claus bake? I hope she bakes some chocolate chip cookies. I absolutely love them! Again thank you for the presents!
Love,
Judith Samantha
(P.S. I was good this year!)

SANTA ENTERPRISES
NORTH POLE

Dear Judith,

You've asked an interesting question. How many elves do I have in my workshop? It may surprise you to know that the answer to that question is: just one. Hard to believe, I know. In fact, at one time I had well in excess of 116,000 elves. But as the centuries progressed, they got it into their heads that they were the all-important cog in the whole North Pole operation, and they began to make increasingly outrageous demands. Eleven months off instead of nine, eggnog breaks every hour as opposed to every four hours, that sort of thing.

Initially I conceded to their demands, feeling that my whole venture could collapse without them. In reality, the more I gave into them, the shoddier their work became. If you think the toys your parents describe having got when they were kids sound crappy, this is the main reason why. The elves became drunk with power (not to mention the eggnog) and felt that they could behave any way they wanted, because they now perceived themselves as having the upper hand. And for a while I assumed they did. Then I discovered China, and I promptly fired those lazy-ass elves—all several hundred thousand of them. I believe most of them are working as garden gnomes, which I'm sure you've noticed have exploded in popularity over the past decade. Now you know why.

As I mentioned, I did keep one elf for publicity and photo purposes. I affectionately call him Scab—but I doubt anyone will be writing any songs about him.

Outsourcingly yours,

Dear Father Christmas,
I have been very good all year. What is it that you would like for Christmas?
Your chum,
Nigel, 10 years old

Dear Nigel,

Why, thank you!

In all the millions of letters I've received over the centuries requesting this and demanding that, no one has ever once asked me what I would like—until now. What I would like is a pair of knickers that don't crawl up my arse when I'm dropping down a chimney. I don't want to have to see that creepy Mr. Bean ever again. I want stupid people to stop voting. I'd like a retirement age that comes sooner than my 750th birthday. I'd like Coca Cola to stop using my image in adverts since I only drink Diet Pepsi. And I'd like half a quid for every copy of *The Night Before Christmas* that is sold.

And since you were kind enough to ask, I'm going to be bringing you everything you want this Christmas—despite your lie about being good all year.

Manners do matter,

FATHER CHRISTMAS

Dear Satan,
Could you take back my little sister? I know I asked for one last year, and though she arrived after Christmas, I still think you brought her for me. She stinks up my room and drools on everything. Oliver down the street has a dog that does the same thing, so I wondered if you could take Julia back and get me a dog? (I already asked my parents if this was okay and they didn't say anything, so that means YES.)
Thanks!
Your pal,
Toby

SANTA ENTERPRISES
NORTH POLE

Dear Toby,

Apparently this letter that you intended for Satan, got mailed to me by mistake. While I'm not completely familiar with how his operation works, I do believe one of his specialties is taking people away—or at least their souls. So while I can't guarantee your request will be successful, the chances are far better than they are asking me.

Good luck!

SANTA

(And no, I don't have Satan's address. Try writing to Dick Cheney, his representative here on Earth.)

Dear Mr. Santa Claus,

We don't celebrate Christmas—we have Hanukah because we are Jewish people. But my teacher said we all have to write to you and my mom didn't answer the phone when the principPAL (he makes us write it that way) called her, so now I have to do what the teacher says.

I don't know you. I see you at all the malls and sometimes I see a menorah nearby. I get presents for 7 days which would be better for you so you don't have to do it all at one night. But I don't know if the reindeer would last. Wouldn't you like more time to get around? You'd have cookies for a week instead of all on one night. You could share them with other people as you travel round.

Teacher says I have to ask for something. I asked to stop having to be writing but she got mad.

May I please get a new model for my spaceship collection? (I said "please".) I hang my spaceships from my room and they glow in the dark at night.

Elliot says I wrote more than the guy at the mall can read, so I guess I'll be stopping now.

Thank you.

Evan Michael 8

P.S.—If my mom writes to you all mad, you can tell her its Mrs. Henley's fault

SANTA ENTERPRISES
NORTH POLE

Dear Evan,

I'm sorry you're stuck in such a crackpot school (next time you write the word principal try spelling it my way—princiPUTZ) and I'm sorry that they made you abase your own religion by writing to me. I know it can't be easy dealing with all the glitz and glamour of Christmas, while pretending you're having just as good of a time with a holiday that isn't even remotely as much fun. But I admire the Jews in how they manage to profit so nicely from the hysteria of the *goyim* at this time of year.

You're obviously an intelligent kid, and have a clear eye for the reality around you. This will pay off for you big time when you grow up and start manufacturing loads of crappy Christmas product for your gentile neighbors to waste even more of their money on.

L'chaim!

SANTA

Dear Santa,

I want a new bike for Christmas. I don't want a train set, a remote control car, or a puppy. You don't need to bring me any toy guns, video games, or rollerblades. I don't need any books or savings bonds. I need a BIKE! And if you could make it either blue, or red, or black that would be cool. Anything but yellow!!!

Thank you, Santa. You're the best.

Bye,

Robbie McNulty

P.S. Remember, a bike!! That's all!

Dear Robbie,

Well, those are a lot of things to remember but don't worry, I have them all logged into our new computerized gift system. It's infallible! So don't worry, this year you'll be getting a train set, a remote control car, a puppy, toy guns, video games, rollerblades, books and savings bonds. Was there anything else? Nope?

Enjoy!

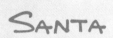

Dear Santa,

Hi, how are you? My best friend Saffron said that we could both write to you and ask for different things that we both want and then we could share. I hope that is okay. (I have to share with my sister all the time and she's always in the bathroom!)

I would like a set of Pony Dolls. Not the little ones with the blue hair, but the ones that look real and can hurt someone if I throw them. I marked a page in the Christmas catalog so you could see what they look like but you and your elves can make them any color (real) that you want.

Now please remember that Saffron is going to ask for these horses too, but you need to get her something else! (She's the one who throws them at her brothers, not me.)

Your dearest friend,

Elyssa

Dear Elyssa,

How stupid do you think I am? I know that you're only trying to pre-vent Saffron from getting Pony Dolls so that you can lord it over her that you have them and she doesn't. I also know that you don't even like the things (except for their ability to inflict pain), and are only making this deceitful attempt for the sole purpose of denying them to Saffron. Well, your nasty little plan isn't going to work. I'll be bringing Saffron every item available in the Pony Dolls line, and the first time you show up after Christmas, her brothers will throw so many horses your way, you'll think you're Catherine the Great. It would pay for you to remember that:

I know when you've been lying,
I know when you're a creep

—or whatever the hell the lines of that song are.

Saddle up!

SANTA

Dear Santa Claus,

Hi!!!!! My name is Saffron and my best friend ever is Elyssa and we're both writing to you to ask for different things that we can share. My brothers steal my toys all the time and when dad makes them give them back they're broken or messed up.

That's why I'm writing you and asking for a Pony Dolls. They don't break no matter how hard my brothers throw them.

Elyssa said she would be asking you for a motor car—Elyssa and me can both ride in it at the same time and my dad can walk behind us. We promise not to go off the sidewalk! Can you bring her a pink one? Purple is OK too!!!!!!!!!!!

Remember, Elyssa gets the car and I get the Pony Dolls, but we promise to share. So that's like getting more presents from you with less work on your part.

I'm going to put this letter in the box at the post office and Elyssa is taking her letter to the mall, so I hope you get both of them!!!

Thank you!

Sincelery,

Your friend,

Saffron (not Elyssa)

SANTA ENTERPRISES
NORTH POLE

Dear Saffron (not Elyssa),

One of the most important lessons to learn in life is how to choose
your friends. So far, you have failed this test miserably.

Try again,

Santa Claus,

Hi! How are you? Remember when I told you I wanted a baby brother or sister last year? It was very nice of you to send me 6, but that's an awful many babies and I thought maybe some other little girl would want one of them this year. So FEEL FREE to take them back at least a few. Mommy said the bunk beds in my room are an early present from you, but I didn't ask for them, but thank you anyway. I want a bigger bed so they know it's not for them. Do you remember them? Jennifer, Jonah, Julia, Jasmine, Jacks, Jordan. They all have the same birthday too. My room is too small for all of us but Daddy doesn't want to put them in the garage and they can't go where his marital arts mats are in the basement.

Maybe I could go in the garage? If you get me a bigger bed, we could put it there and put the big van outside. I wouldn't mind. Anyway. You were very nice to send so many babies but maybe someone else wants them now?

And a doll that looks like Hannah Montana but isn't because Mommy doesn't like her.

TY! <—that means THANK YOU

Love,

Jodie Jo

Dear Jodie Jo,

Clearly, your father needs to put away his "marital" arts mats in the basement, since he has obviously made too much use of them. Either that or your mom's fertility drug dosage leaned a little on the heavy side. Or maybe you just don't know how to spell. In any case, your mother is right about Hannah Montana. She could be in rehab before you reach junior high. But you should be nice to your six new siblings. By the time they're seven, they'll have their own top-rated cable series, *The Sensational Sextuplets*. The Disney Channel will be thrilled to have finally gotten the word "sex" into the title of one of their programs, and the ratings will be off the charts until your siblings become *passé* at puberty.

It's All Karma, Baby.

Santa Claus,

I want a very cool spaceship. Last Christmas you brought me the same one you gave to Toby in my class. But everyone knows he chews on his toys, so I want one that he can't play with when he comes over. I'll take very good care of it if you do. Mum says the one I want is too expensive for you, but I know your elfs make the toys, not buy them so what does it cost? Nothing.

(Sides, my mum showed my dad some necklace she wants and I saw it on the telly and it's very much money too. Can you make a cheaper one for her?) Okay. Thanks for your time, sir. I hope you have a nice day.

Sincerely,

Ian

Dear Ian,

What happened to the spaceship I gave you last year? Of course I know exactly where you disposed of it, but I was hoping you'd have the decency to make mention of it. I fail to see how the fact that Toby chewed on his (I really do need to start looking into the lead content on those things) has anything to do with your spaceship. You had the opportunity to take good care of that one and failed miserably at the task. Whatever made you even think that petrol could make a good rocket fuel?

I also think it's wonderful how you're willing to sell out your mother's gift for the sake of your own. What a loving child you are. Perhaps when she receives exactly what she's hoping for, and you receive the charred remains of last year's spaceship, it will make you pause and consider your behavior.

G'day mate,

Dear Santa,

I would like a different dad this year. Mommy got one when I was at camp last summer and now Eddie's here all the time. His car smells and he calls me "buddy" and rubs my hair. I asked Mommy if we could get a different one and she made this face and went out of the room.

I thought maybe you could bring Mr. Wade from science class. Drew's big brother has him for biology and says he could use a date. I'm sure my mom would give him one. She met him at some PTA thing last year and talks about him all the time. But when I asked her if he could be my dad, she said he wasn't going to get married. I don't know what that has to do with anything. But I know he doesn't pat my head and mess up my hair. He's very clean and that's important, right? RIGHT?

OK so you take Eddie and bring Mr. Wade I don't know his first name. We could call him Steve, that's a nice name OK?

Then I can play with the race cars you gave me last year and you won't have to bring me any other toys. We all win!

Thank you for your time.

Aldon

Dear Aldon,

I'm afraid I haven't brought another human being as a gift for someone since the Universal Declaration of Human Rights was ratified
back in the late 1940's. (I'll admit I held off for years before finally
signing it. But when it came down to just me and my ally China as
the final holdouts, I conceded the point and added my signature.)

I will give you something even better, though, and that's a sure-fire
way to get rid of your mom's current boyfriend. Next time you no-
tice that funny smell in Eddie's car, just dial 911 and give his name
and license plate number to the operator. You won't have to see him
again for a long, long time.

I'm afraid that Mr. Wade won't make a good replacement, though.
While he would be a wonderful father for you, I'm afraid he
wouldn't make a very good husband for your mom. He doesn't really
like girls, if you know what I mean. But don't worry, your mom will
find someone perfect for both of you eventually.

Assuredly yours,

Dearest Santa Claus,
I want a Barbie, a dollhouse not the pink
one but the one with the elevator, a set of
magic tricks, a basketball, pink boots, a gift
card to the toy store, a High School Musical
sweatshirt like Ally's, a dvd player, and for
you to come back in the summer when I can
stay up later and meet you
Thank you
Natalie

Dear Natalie,

What makes you think I have any interest in meeting you? And why does Barbie need an elevator? The stairs are a great way for her to keep that famous figure of hers. If you put in a little time on the stairs you also wouldn't need that enormous *High School Musical* sweatshirt, either. Not that I'm one to talk in that regard, but I also don't have any desire to bag Zac Efron for a boyfriend.

Keep sweatin',

Santa,

'Supp? That means "what's up", get it? It means your a cool dude and I'm cool too so we can be cool together. I bet your very cool in the north pole hahahaha!

I saw the picture of the polar bear on the ice melting and wondered if that would happen to you? Will the elves float away? Where will they go? Do you know they club seals sometimes? That's not cool, but I want to see it happen. Answer me about the ice because dad says it won't bother you and mommy says it will.

For Xmas I want a video game station with TWO controllers, a flight game, the car stealing game, and the one with the zombies in the mall. I play it at Javier's house and his mom lets us. I also want a football jersey but only from a player who is nice to his dog. I watch football on TV. Do you watch football? Do you know why it's called a football? Because it's a ball you kick with your foot to make a goal! Get it?

I have another joke for you: what did one reindeer say to the other reindeer? Sure does smell around here! Hahahahahaha!

Bye,

Declan

Dear Declan,

Your attempt to be gangsta would merely be tiresome if you were actually black. The fact that you're a pasty-faced white kid just makes it laughable. And it's clearly the only laugh you'll get based on your joke-telling ability.

You do bring up a good point about global warming, though, and what that means for me. Your mother is right, and you father is obviously a douche bag, or a Republican (or most likely, both). He would only need to look at a map to see why I'm concerned. There is no LAND at the North Pole! If the ice melts, my whole operation sinks into the Arctic Ocean. Thankfully, I'm prepared. A fallback facility is currently under construction at the South Pole, even as we speak. But don't you worry. Just keep playing your car theft games even as the water creeps up to your knees.

Hope you can swim!

SANTA

PS: And despite all the negative accusations I can make about my former elves, the clubbing of seals is not one of them. That would have required effort on their part.

Dear Santa,

How are you and Mrs. Santa and Rudolph? I have been good — well, most of the time anyway. I would like it a lot if you could come to my house on Christmas Eve and bring with you a bus and an ambulance and a truck and a train and some legos and a Frosty the Snowman toy and a new toothbrush. Also, can you bring my brother, Joshua, a pillowcase filled with money?

Thanks very much. I'll look for you on Christmas Eve and leave you cookies.

Love,

Baz (Sebastian)

Dear Baz,

Just how much do you think I can fit into my bag, for Chrissakes? While I know the obvious thing would be to assume you meant a TOY bus, ambulance, truck and train, I know that you actually expect working, full-size vehicles. Well, that's not going to happen. Your brother is being far more practical in asking for a pillowcase filled with money. Not that that's going to happen either. I used to bring kids cash, which I printed myself, until I fell afoul of the international crime bureaus of any number of countries. Scotland Yard came close to almost launching a full-scale assault on the North Pole. Well, I learned my lesson, by gum. Now I just slip my counterfeit pounds, euros, pesos and dollars into the world's economy in small untraceable amounts. My condo in the Caymans is a perfect location for both some much needed off-season R&R and an ideal place to infuse capital into my operation.

Of course now that I've told you all of this, I'm afraid I'll have to eliminate you.

Ha ha! Just kidding.

SANTA

Dear (and I use that term loosely) Santa,
It is now clear to me that you are a rightwing
nutcracker who is not at all interested in world
peace, since I have been ASKING you for world
peace for almost forty years. Every single time someone
asks you to fulfill some materialistic whim, you're down
that chimney in a heartbeat. For the love of God, just
how many iPod Nano's does this world need? But when
people ask for the real things— an end to global
warming, war, poverty, and injustice—you're dancing on
the roof with that violinist or I don't know what.
You're nothing but a shill for product placement—some
company even provides your wardrobe. If you bring me
one more gift card for a store I would rather burn to
the ground than shop in, you'll find it placed where not
even coal could bring forth light.
Sincerely,
Nancy

SANTA ENTERPRISES
NORTH POLE

Dear Nancy,

I am neither rightwing, nor leftwing. What I am is anti-authority. For the last eight years I have been against your country's Republican party, which has proven itself to be base, profligate, venal, criminal, arrogant, evil, corrupt and yet still utterly incompetent. This previously unimaginable combination of adjectives has set a standard so repulsively low, that it will be centuries before another administration comes close to matching it. Sadly, as the pendulum swings toward your Democratic party, I'll soon be repulsed by the return to a whiny, self-righteous, micro-managing attempt at regulating every aspect of life.

Which brings me to your letter. Has it ever occurred to you that I bring people iPod Nanos and not world peace because the first is within my power and the second is not? In the fairy tale world you see yourself inhabiting, where everybody watches solar-powered public television and wipes their ass with leaves, I guarantee it's only a matter of time before you begin fighting amongst yourselves over how to handle the exploding population of disease-ridden deer that have now inundated your hippy-dippy vegan society.

Human civilization continues to advance because people are inherently dissatisfied. From dissatisfaction springs progress in science and medicine, and every other aspect of life. Unfortunately, this same characteristic generates greed, war and injustice. The same human trait that strives to develop pollution-free energy also strives to racially purify Darfur. It's ultimately *your* job to encourage the positive aspect of this trait while discouraging the negative. So get off your self-righteous ass and stop laying this one at my doorstep.

Talk is cheap,

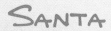

Dear Father Christmas,
I want just ONE thing. Each year you bring me lots
and lots of Leeds United stuff, which I really am
thankful for, but then you never let my team
actually win. This year you don't have to bring me
any footballs or shirts or pennants or posters or
anything with my team's name on it. All I want this
year is for you to let Leeds United win.
Signed
Neville

Dear Neville,

Honestly, I have no control over which teams actually win. If I did, I would have made a fortune betting on them over the years, and wouldn't be breaking my back hauling toys around every Christmas. Whatever power granted me the ability to see much of the future, and to know who is naughty and nice, appears to have played a cruel joke by not allowing me to see anything that I could potentially gamble on. And frankly, the sad truth is that Leeds United is bloody awful and will be for the foreseeable future. I don't need a crystal ball to see that.

On the other hand, you could consider moving to Manchester.

Keep the faith!

FATHER CHRISTMAS

Dear Santa Claus,

All I want for Christmas is my two front teeth. I know your fake, everyone at school knows you're fake. How come nobody ever sees you? I always try to stay awake, but I never seen you. How come you never eat all the cookies my mom makes? How come I never get everything I want from you? I don't think that raindeer can fly. And you can't fit down my chimney. Haley dosent have a chimney. Britney knows the tooth fairy is fake she saw her dad put money under her pillow. And Danny knows the easter bunny is fake because he's jewish. So I'm just gonna give you this stupid letter when your at the mall and you better just give me vampire teeth or else I know for sure. I been really nice all year.

Noah, 10

Dear Noah,

I'm not about to spill the beans about the Tooth Fairy—or the Easter Bunny for that matter. (Although I can vouch for him that he is definitely not Jewish. The Jews control Valentine's Day and have lately been muscling in on Arbor Day, but they steer clear of Easter for obvious reasons.) Regardless, I'm glad to see that you and you're friends are already becoming bitter and cynical at the ripe old age of ten. Go right ahead and sap the joy and wonder out of your lives. The sooner you become dull, unimaginative drones, the sooner you can take your places as cogs in the dreary service economy that is taking over your country and sucking the life-blood from your very soul.

I agree that vampire teeth represent the perfect gift for you this year.

You suck,